Learning With Numbers

BREAD and CEREAL

to Grow On

by

Doris Cambruzzi and Claire Thornton

illustrations by Lorraine Arthur

STANDARD PUBLISHING

Cincinnati, Ohio　　　3609

This is my book.

My name is _____ .

Library of Congress Catalog Card Number 86-060739
ISBN 0-87403-129-X

Dear Parent:

God, our loving Father, has entrusted our children to us, to guide and direct in both spiritual and bodily growth here on earth. This book is designed to help your children become familiar with good nutrition so that they will eat the correct foods for a healthy body.

Nutrition pertains to what we eat and how our bodies use it. Essential nutrients must be obtained from the foods we eat. Protein, carbohydrates, fat, vitamins, minerals, and water are the six classes of essential nutrients we obtain from our diets.

Whether we eat at home or we eat out, we are faced with important food choices. Children's needs change with age. One set of rules simply cannot apply to everyone. There is a practical guide to good nutrition, which translates the technical knowledge of nutrition into a plan for everyday eating. This guide, "The Four Food Groups," provides the kind and quantity of food necessary for a balanced diet. The Four Food Groups are Fruit-Vegetable Group, Meat Group, Milk Group, and Bread-Cereal Group.

A key to good health is to eat a variety of foods from each of the four food groups every day and get proper rest and exercise. It is very important to start your young children with good health habits.

Why do some people accept some foods and reject others? A primary factor in food acceptance seems to be the training of the young child in familiarity with a wide variety of foods. This training should be started at an early age, supported both in the home and by effective educational experiences.

Coauthor Doris Cambruzzi conducted a study on this subject and found that education, in addition to the provision of food, was an important factor in the vegetable consumption practices of children. The pattern of eating established during early childhood is believed to affect food choice and, to some extent, nutritional status throughout life.

This book is a learning aid to help your child become familiar with foods from the Bread-Cereal Group and to understand the correct portion that is needed by the body, which is the key to weight control throughout life. The illustrations of bread, cereal, and grains contained in this book will help children identify them, and the recipes are easy and fun.

—Doris Cambruzzi
—Claire Thornton

EAT A VARIETY OF FOODS FROM

MILK GROUP

Drink or eat 2 to 3 servings daily of foods from the Milk Group if you are under age 9. This group is a primary source of calcium. It also gives us phosphorous, riboflavin (vitamin B_2), and complete protein.

One serving from the
Milk Group

= 1 cup (8 ounces) of milk
= 1½ ounces of cheese
= 1¾ cups of ice cream
= 2 cups of cottage cheese
= 1 cup of yogurt

MEAT GROUP

Eat 2 or more servings daily of foods from the Meat Group. Foods in this group supply protein and iron and are a good source of the B vitamins.

One serving from the
Meat Group

= 2 or 3 ounces of cooked meat, poultry, or fish
= 2 eggs
= 1 cup of dry beans, peas, or lentils, cooked
= 4 tablespoons of peanut butter

THE FOUR FOOD GROUPS!

FRUIT-VEGETABLE
GROUP

Eat 4 or more servings each day from the Fruit-Vegetable Group.

Foods in this group supply most of our daily needs for vitamin C and vitamin A. Fiber is present in all fruits and vegetables, especially in the skins.

One serving from the
Fruit-Vegetable Group
= ½ cup of a fruit or vegetable, or a portion as ordinarily served such as 1 medium banana

BREAD-CEREAL
GROUP

Turn the page and have fun with the Bread-Cereal Group.

God made us, and God made the food we eat. God made the land and the sea, the sun and the moon, the rain and the air around us, and all the animals and plants for us to enjoy.

Bread and cereal are some of the foods that God gave us to eat. They taste good and are good for us.

God wants us to have healthy bodies and to take good care of our bodies. When we eat the right foods, we grow and feel good; and when we feel good, we can serve Him better.

This book tells you about bread and cereal, and gives you some recipes so that you can enjoy eating them in different ways. You will also learn more about counting and numbers.

Have fun eating foods from the Bread and Cereal Group; they will help you stay healthy!

Bread and Cereal Group

The foods in this group come from grains and are a good source of thiamin (vitamin B_1), niacin, and iron, a mineral our bodies need.

These foods also supply us with carbohydrates and some protein.

Whole grains contain fiber, which is good for us.

Eat 4 or more servings each day from the Bread-Cereal Group.

One serving from the Bread-Cereal Group
= 1 slice of bread
= 1 ounce of ready-to-eat cereal
= ½ to ¾ cup of cooked cereal, macaroni, rice, grits, or spaghetti

Farmers grow these grains in their fields.
Then the grains are made into the bread and cereal
products that you see when you go shopping.

GRAINS

There are 7 common grains that belong to the Bread and Cereal Group:

Whole grain products are good for us because they have more trace minerals than refined products.

Foods that are made from refined flour should be enriched or fortified to replace or add vitamins and minerals that are lost in the refining process.

1 ONE

The farmer grows grain.
Grain is made into flour.
Flour is made into bread.

French Toast

4 slices of bread
2 eggs
¼ cup of milk
⅛ teaspoon salt
½ teaspoon vanilla
1 tablespoon butter or margarine

Break the eggs into a flat bowl.
Add the milk, salt, and vanilla.
Mix well with a fork or eggbeater.
Put a skillet on the stove over medium heat.
As soon as the skillet is hot, add the butter, spreading it as it melts.
Lay each slice of bread in the egg mixture and soak it.
Then place the soaked bread into the skillet and brown first on one side and then the other.
Serve with butter and confectioner's sugar mixed with cinnamon.
Add syrup or applesauce on top.
Makes 4 servings.

1 piece of French Toast = 1 serving from the Bread and
Cereal Group

2 TWO

Pancake mix has flour in it.
Flour comes from grain.

Animal Pancakes

1 cup pancake mix
1 cup milk
1 egg
1 tablespoon melted butter or margarine
Crumbled bacon or raisins (optional)

Mix pancakes according to the directions on the box of pancake mix.

Lightly grease the griddle.

Using a spoon, pour batter onto griddle and form animal shapes. (Or pour batter into open cookie cutters. Or, if you wish, make round pancakes and cut with animal cookie cutters.)

Turn pancakes when tops are covered with bubbles.

Decorate with bacon bits or raisins to make faces for animals.

Serve with syrup if desired.

Makes 6 servings.

3 THREE

Hot cereal is good for you.
Cereal comes from grains like wheat, oats, rice, and corn.

Hot Oatmeal

1 cup rolled oats
2 cups water
Cinnamon, chopped nuts, and fruit, optional

Bring water to a boil in a pan.

Add oats and a dash of salt.

Let the oatmeal mixture boil again, then turn the stove down to low, cover the pan, and cook for about 10 to 12 minutes.

If using instant oats, follow directions on package.

Cinnamon, chopped nuts, or fruit such as chopped apples or raisins may be added during cooking time.

Makes 4 cups cooked cereal.

Cleanup Tip: For easy cleanup, fill the pan with cold water after cereal is served.

4 FOUR

Crackers are made from flour that comes from grains.

What are your favorite crackers?
  Soda crackers?
  Graham crackers?
  Rye crackers?
  Whole-wheat crackers?
  Fun-shaped snack crackers?

Here is a recipe for you to make your own crackers.

Cheese Crackers

1 cup grated Cheddar cheese
¼ cup softened butter
¼ teaspoon celery seed
¼ teaspoon salt
¼ teaspoon onion
½ cup sifted flour

Mix all ingredients together and roll out.
Cut into squares.
Bake in the oven at 450 degrees for about 8 minutes.
Makes about 18 crackers.

5 FIVE

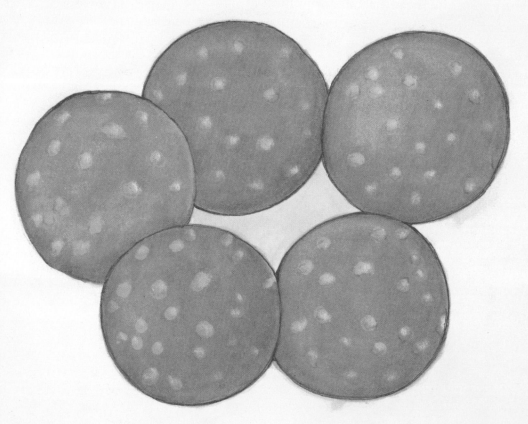

Breakfast Take Alongs are high-protein cookies that you can eat with a glass of milk and get the nutrients your body needs at breakfasttime.

Breakfast Take Alongs

⅔ cup butter or margarine
⅔ cup sugar
1 egg
1 teaspoon vanilla
¾ cup all-purpose flour
½ teaspoon soda
½ teaspoon salt
1½ cups quick or old-fashioned uncooked oatmeal
1 cup (4 ounces) shredded Cheddar cheese
½ cup wheat germ or finely chopped nuts

Beat together butter, sugar, egg, and vanilla until well-blended.

Add combined flour, soda, and salt; mix well.

Stir in oats, cheese, and wheat germ.

Drop by rounded tablespoonfuls onto greased cookie sheet.

Bake in preheated 350 degree oven 12 to 14 minutes, or until edges are golden brown.

Cool 1 minute on cookie sheet; remove to wire cooling rack.

Store in loosely covered container in refrigerator or at room temperature.

Breakfast is important.
It gives you the energy to run and play and feel good.
Do NOT skip breakfast.

6 SIX

Six is half a dozen.
Muffins are good for a morning or afternoon snack.

Bran Cereal Muffins

1 cup whole-bran cereal
1 cup milk
1 egg
¼ cup oil
¼ cup honey
1¼ cups whole-wheat flour
2 teaspoons baking powder
¼ teaspoon baking soda
½ teaspoon salt

Preheat oven to 400 degrees.
Grease muffin tins.
Stir the bran cereal and milk together in a bowl and let it stand for 2 minutes.
Add egg, oil, and honey. Beat the mixture until it is well-blended.
Mix the remaining dry ingredients together, then add them to the bran mixture.
Stir until just mixed; do not over beat.
Pour the mixture into the muffin tins.
Bake about 20 to 25 minutes or until lightly browned.
Makes 12 muffins.

7 SEVEN

Store grains in tight containers in a cool place. To retain freshness, refrigerate or freeze.

To cook grains, bring a large pot of water to a boil and add the grain. Stir once and when the water returns to a boil, turn the heat down to low, cover the pot, and let the grain cook until done, about 30 to 40 minutes.

Boiled Rice

½ cup rice
1 cup water
½ teaspoon salt

Put the water into a large saucepan. Add the salt.

Bring the water to a boil over medium heat.

Dribble the rice into the boiling water so that the bubbling does not stop.

Reduce heat and cook for 15 to 20 minutes until the rice is tender and water is absorbed.

Serve hot with butter, salt, and pepper, or cold with cream and sugar.

Caramel Rice Pudding

2 cups cooked rice
1¼ cups milk
⅛ teaspoon salt
1 tablespoon butter

1 teaspoon vanilla
½ cup brown sugar
2 eggs
¼ cup raisins

Take the butter out of the refrigerator ahead of time so that it is soft enough to blend with the other ingredients.

Break the eggs into a large bowl.

Add the milk, salt, butter, vanilla, and brown sugar.

Beat with a fork until all ingredients are well mixed.

Add the cooked rice and the raisins, stirring gently to mix well.

Pour the mixture into a greased baking dish.

Bake in a 325 degree oven for 30 minutes.

When cool, serve either plain or with milk.

Macaroni and Cheese

1½ cups elbow macaroni
¾ cup milk
1½ cups grated sharp Cheddar cheese*
2 tablespoons butter
Salt and pepper

Cook macaroni according to directions on package. Drain macaroni in a colander.
Preheat oven to 350 degrees.
Mix all ingredients together in a baking dish.
Bake in oven at 350 degrees for 30 minutes.
Makes 6 servings.

*If you do not have packaged cheese, you can grate your own. Put waxed paper under the grater, and grate cheese until you have 1½ cups.

Spaghetti

1 pound package spaghetti
1 pound ground beef
1 large jar spaghetti sauce
Butter, salt, and pepper (optional)

Brown ground beef in large skillet or large heavy pan. Drain off excess fat.
Add sauce and heat through.
Cook spaghetti in large pot according to directions on package. Drain spaghetti in a colander.
Return to pot and toss with butter, salt, and pepper, if desired.
Serve heated sauce over spaghetti on each plate.
Serves 6.

8 EIGHT

People around the world eat different kinds of bread.
Tacos are a kind of bread made from corn.

Beef Tacos

12 taco shells, fully
  cooked
1 pound ground beef
¼ cup chopped onion
1 8-ounce can tomato
  sauce
2 teaspoons chili powder
1 cup chopped tomato
1 cup shredded lettuce
½ cup natural sharp Cheddar cheese, shredded (2
  ounces)
Taco sauce, as desired

Heat taco shells as directed on package.

Brown ground beef and onion in a frying pan. Drain
off excess fat.

Stir in tomato sauce and chili powder.

Bring to a boil. Reduce heat.

Cook 10 to 15 minutes uncovered, stirring occasion-
ally until mixture is dry and crumbly.

Fill heated taco shells with 2 tablespoons meat mixture.

Mix tomato, lettuce, and cheese. Spoon 2 tablespoons
over beef in taco shells. Or keep ingredients in separate
bowls and let people create their own tacos.

Drizzle with taco sauce, as desired.

9 NINE

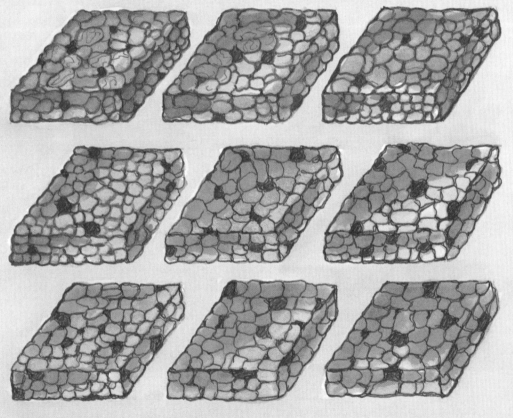

Granola bars are made with oats.
They are full of nutrients that give you energy.
They are good as snacks between meals.

Granola Bars

3½ cups quick or old-fashioned oats, uncooked
1¼ cups raisins
¾ cup chopped nuts
⅔ cup butter or margarine, melted
½ cup brown sugar, firmly packed
⅓ cup honey or molasses
1 egg, beaten
1 teaspoon vanilla
¼ teaspoon salt

Toast oats in a large ungreased shallow baking pan in a preheated oven at 350 degrees for 15 to 20 minutes.

Combine the toasted oats in a large bowl with the rest of the ingredients, and mix well.

Press firmly into a well-greased 13″ x 9″ pan.

Bake in a 350 degree oven for about 20 minutes.

Cool; cut into bars.

Makes 24 to 36 squares.

10 TEN

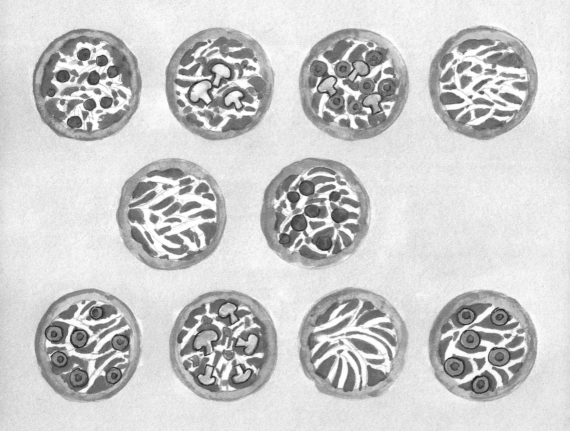

Pizza crust is part of the Bread and Cereal Group.

Pizza

10 refrigerator biscuits, flaky, 9½ ounce package
¼ cup tomato paste
1 teaspoon oregano
¼ cup chopped onion
⅓ cup chopped mushrooms, canned or fresh
½ cup shredded mozzarella cheese

Preheat oven to 400 degrees.

Grease 2 baking sheets.

Pat each biscuit round into a 4-inch circle on baking sheet.

Mix tomato paste and oregano, and spread it on each biscuit round.

Mix onion and mushrooms and sprinkle over tomato paste mixture.*

Top with shredded mozzarella cheese.

Bake about 8 minutes until crust is lightly browned.

Makes 10 small pizzas.

*Other favorite pizza garnishes may be added also.

We thank You, God, for bread and cereal
to grow on. Amen.